Violin Exam Pieces

ABRSM Grade 3

Selected from the 2012–2015 syllabus

Name

Date of exam

Violin & Piano   Piano only

Contents

page

Violin consultant: Philippa Bunting
Footnotes: Edward Huws Jones (EHJ), Richard Jones (RJ) and Anthony Burton

Other pieces for Grade 3

First published in 2011 by ABRSM (Publishing) Ltd, a wholly owned subsidiary of ABRSM, 24 Portland Place, London W1B 1LU, United Kingdom

© 2011 by The Associated Board of the Royal Schools of Music

Music origination by Andrew Jones
Cover by Økvik Design
Printed in England by Halstan & Co. Ltd, Amersham, Bucks.

2

La Rotta

Arranged by Edward Huws Jones

Anon. 14th-century Italian

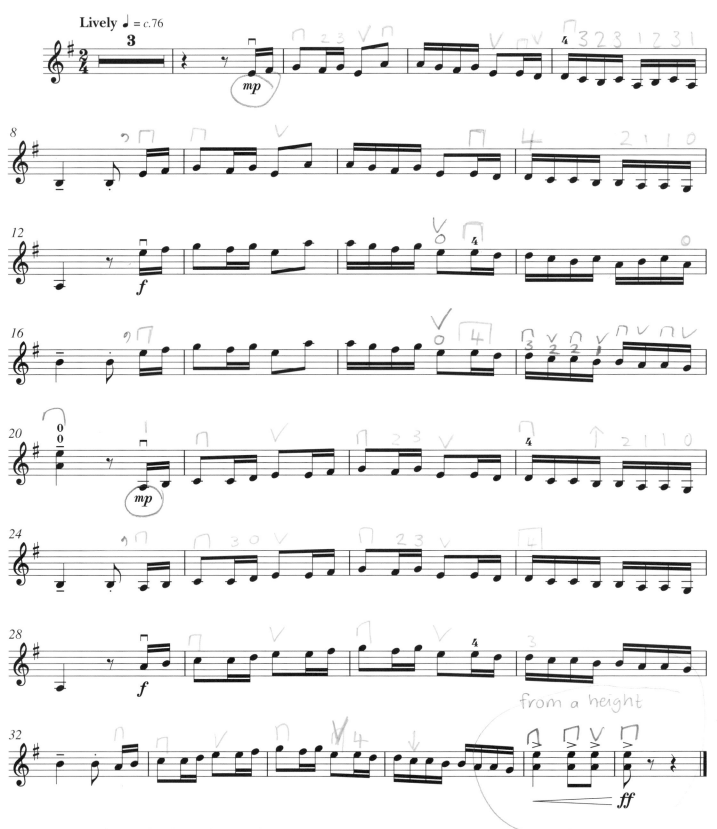

La Rotta is a dance from medieval Italy. The original manuscript gives only the melody, without accompaniment. This arrangement suggests a folky style; think of drones and rhythmic percussion. EHJ

Gavotta

Fourth movement from Sonata in F, Op. 5 No. 10

A:2

Edited by and continuo realized by
Richard Jones

Arcangelo Corelli

The Italian composer Arcangelo Corelli (1653–1713) studied in Bologna as a young man, and in the 1670s moved to Rome, where he achieved great fame as a violinist, composer, teacher and orchestral director. In the 18th century his sonatas and concertos were revered as models owing to the classical purity of their style.

This gavotta is taken from the celebrated set of 12 Violin Sonatas, Op. 5, which Corelli dedicated to the Electress Sophie Charlotte of Brandenburg in 1700. They became the most influential violin sonatas of the 18th century: Charles Burney remarked, in his *A General History of Music* of 1789, that these were the sonatas 'on which all good schools for the violin have since been founded'.

The 'gavotta', the Italian version of the French gavotte, is a moderately fast, light-hearted dance in duple or quadruple time. According to the flautist and theorist J. J. Quantz, it should be played 'with a short and light bow-stroke'. The repeats, indicated by repeat marks in the original, are here written out in full. The dynamics, the slurs in bars 11 and 15, and the trills and their slurs are editorial suggestions only. RJ

Source: *Sonate a violino e violone o cimbalo*, Op. 5 (Rome, 1700)

An Chloë

K. 524

Arranged by Lionel Salter

W. A. Mozart

An Chloë To Chloë

Wolfgang Amadeus Mozart (1756–91) was born in the Austrian city of Salzburg, but spent the last ten years of his short life in Vienna, the capital of the Austro-Hungarian Empire. He is famous for his operas, symphonies and concertos, but his songs are less well known. This is an adaptation of the first part of his song *An Chloë*, sometimes known by its first line, 'Wenn die Lieb'' (it begins 'When love shines out of your bright blue eyes…'). According to his own handwritten catalogue of his works, Mozart wrote the song in Vienna on 24 June 1787 – just before the well-known *Eine kleine Nachtmusik* for strings, and while he was also working on the opera *Don Giovanni*. Its apparent simplicity conceals some subtle variations in the length of phrases.

Theme from *Le streghe*

Op. 8

Arranged by Shin'ichi Suzuki

Nicolò Paganini

B:1

Le streghe The Witches

Nicolò Paganini (1782–1840), a native of the Italian city of Genoa, was the most famous violinist of his age: his brilliant performances created a sensation in concert halls all over Europe. His compositions include *Le streghe*, written in 1813 as a piece for violin and orchestra but not published in his lifetime – perhaps so that he could keep its technical secrets to himself. It consists of an introduction and a set of variations on a melody from a ballet score by Mozart's pupil Franz Xaver Süssmayr (1766–1803), taken from a scene in which witches gather round a magic nut tree. This is a free adaptation of the theme alone made by Shin'ichi Suzuki (1898–1998), the Japanese inventor of the Suzuki system of musical education.

B:2

Ständchen

from *Schwanengesang*, D. 957

Arranged by Hywel Davies

Franz Schubert

Ständchen Serenade; **Schwanengesang** Swan Song

In his short lifetime, the Austrian composer Franz Schubert (1797–1828) wrote over 600 songs, establishing new standards for the art of setting poetry in German. He wrote his 'Ständchen' towards the end of his life, probably in August 1828; it was included in a collection called *Schwanengesang*, which was published after his death. The poem, by Ludwig Rellstab, is written as if sung by a man to a woman at night underneath her window: 'Softly my songs plead to you through the night; beloved, come down into the quiet grove.' The piano part suggests that the singer is accompanying himself on a guitar or mandolin.

Träumerei

No. 7 from *Kinderscenen*, Op. 15

B:3

Arranged by Lionel Salter

Robert Schumann

Träumerei Reverie; **Kinderscenen** Scenes from Childhood

The German composer Robert Schumann (1810–56) trained to be a pianist, fell in love with and eventually married a celebrated pianist named Clara Wieck, and in the first part of his career wrote almost nothing but music for piano – although later he also composed songs, chamber music, orchestral music, choral music and an opera. His early flood of keyboard music includes a suite of 13 pieces called *Kinderscenen*, written in February and March 1838. It was not primarily intended for children to play, but is a series of impressions of childhood, suggested by a remark of Clara's that sometimes Robert seemed to her 'like a child'. The most famous piece of the set, here arranged for violin and piano, is 'Träumerei': 'Reverie' or 'Dreaming'.

© 1990 by The Associated Board of the Royal Schools of Music

C:1

Puttin' on the Ritz

Arranged by Mary Cohen

Irving Berlin

Irving Berlin (1888–1989) was born in Russia, the son of a cantor in a synagogue, but moved to the United States at the age of five. Despite having no formal musical training, he became one of the most successful American songwriters of the 20th century, writing both the lyrics and the music of numerous hit songs, many of them for Broadway musicals or Hollywood films. He wrote *Puttin' on the Ritz* in 1929 as a single song, but the following year it was featured in a film of the same name. It makes use of syncopated ragtime rhythms, sometimes in unexpected patterns. The title refers to dressing up in style (there were grand Ritz hotels in Paris and London, and a Ritz-Carlton in New York), and is sung to the recurring scale figure in triplet rhythms.

From the motion picture PUTTIN' ON THE RITZ

for my darling boy

Joshi's Dance

C:2

Michael Zev Gordon

The composer Michael Zev Gordon was born in London in 1963, and studied at Cambridge University and in Italy and the Netherlands. He has taught composition in Manchester, Durham and Birmingham, and is now a senior lecturer at the University of Southampton and a professor of composition at the Royal College of Music in London. He has written music for many leading orchestras, ensembles and choirs. Gordon wrote *Joshi's Dance* in March 2009 for a volume in the ABRSM *Spectrum* series, and he says about it: 'This little piece was written for my son Joshi to play. It should sound fun and bouncy in the fast parts and suddenly tender in the slow bars.' The changes of tempo, and the commas before them indicating a slight pause, mean that the violinist will need to lead each new start with an upbeat like a conductor's.

AB 3582

Hungarian Dance

Pál Járdányi

The Hungarian composer Pál Járdányi (1920–66) studied the violin at the Budapest Academy of Music before being admitted to the class of the well-known composer and teacher Zoltán Kodály. While he was still a student, he made his first tour of rural Hungary to collect folksongs, as Kodály and his friend Bartók had done a generation earlier; and like them he became an expert in the subject. In the last few years before his early death, he was head of the department of ethnomusicology (the study of traditional music) at the Budapest Academy of Sciences. This *Hungarian Dance*, an original piece in folk style, was one of Járdányi's contributions to the third volume of a *Violin Tutor* published in 1952, of which he was joint editor.